DIABETIC

MEAL PREP

COOKBOOK

FOR

BEGINNERS

Delicious Recipes to reverse type 1 and 2 diabetics, boost weight loss and ensure total body healing.

DR ANN ORIS

Table of Contents

A diabetic diet is a diet used by people diagnosed with diabetes mellitus or high blood sugar to control long-term blood sugar symptoms and hazardous complications such as cardiovascular or heart diseases, kidney disease and obesity).The most critical aspect of any diet for overweight and obese people with diabetes is that it results in a reduction of fat in the body. Losing body fat has been shown to enhance control over blood glucose and lower insulin levels.

The most widely- accepted recommendation is that the diet must be low in sugar and refined carbohydrates, while the dietary fiber, especially soluble fiber, must be relatively large.

People with diabetes can also be advised to reduce their consumption of high glycemic index (GI) carbohydrates, although the ADA and Diabetes UK state that more evidence is required for this recommendation. However, in cases of hypoglycemia, it is best to have food or drink that can rapidly increase blood glucose, such as a sugar sports drink, accompanied by a long-acting carbohydrate to reduce the risk of hypoglycemia

I realize, as someone struggling with diabetes, that it can be very tough to find equilibrium during the holidays. It is no easy feat to learn and relax up and enjoy yourself, while keeping your blood sugar in check. Yet blood sugar control has never been smooth sailing. For diabetes, looking after your blood sugar is important for long-term wellbeing. It's also the secret to feeling good, remaining strong, and finally being able to let go and enjoy yourself!

I have been able to discover what works best for me to manage and regulate my blood sugar, particularly during the holiday season, during my 11 years of living with type 1 diabetes, with many ups and downs and plenty of trial and error.

Here are some of the delicious and tasty recipes that will assist in the control of both type 1 and type 2 diabetes.

CHARGRILLED VEGETABLE SALAD

Ingredients

- Three tablespoon of olive oil
- Two red pepper
- One teaspoon of red wine vinegar
- One aubergine
- Two red onion (sliced)
- One red chilli
- One small garlic clove (grinded)
- Big sundried tomatoes in oil
- One black olive
- Large black basil, roughly torn.

Instructions

- ✓ Directly over the flame, blackened the pepper all over. Place them in a tub, cover with a plate, and set aside to cool fully.
- ✓ In a big mixing bowl, combine the oil, vinegar, garlic, and chill.
- ✓ Chargrill the onions, aubergine, and courgette in batches on a hot griddle pan until they have grill marks on both sides and are softening. The time limit is unquestionably determined by the temperature of your grill.
- ✓ Put the vegetables in the dressing to marinate as soon as they're ready, breaking up the onions into rings.

✓ Peel the peppers, cut the stalk, and scrape out the seeds when they are cool enough to handle. Slice into strips and toss with the vegetables in the bowl's juice.

ZUCCHINI PANCAKES

Ingredients

- One medium zucchini
- One tablespoon of grated red onion
- Two extra large eggs (lightly beaten)
- Three tablespoons of all purpose flour
- Half tablespoon of ground black pepper

- Half tablespoon salt
- Vegetable oil
- One teaspoon of baking powder

Instructions

- ✓ Preheat the oven to over 300 degrees Fahrenheit.
- ✓ In a mixing bowl, grate the zucchini and add the onions and eggs right away.
- ✓ Combine the flour, baking powder, salt, and pepper in a mixing bowl.
- ✓ Add the vegetable oil to a big sauté pan and steam over medium heat.
- ✓ Reduce the heat to medium low and pour the batter into the pan once the oil is hot. Cook for 2 minutes on either side, or until golden brown.

✓ Place the pancakes in the oven and keep them warm for up to 30 minutes before serving.

CARAMELIZED CARROTS AND ONIONS

Ingredients

- Six whole carrots (cut in a coin form)
- Half whole yellow onion
- Three tablespoon of olive oil
- Water (1\4 cup)
- Three teaspoons of brown sugar
- Two teaspoons of maple syrup /honey
- One teaspoon of butter

Instructions

- ✓ In a pan, heat the oil, then add the onion slices. Set the heat to medium-high and wait for the onions to soften.
- ✓ When the onions begin to brown, season with salt and reduce to medium low heat, stirring periodically for about 12 minutes.
- ✓ As the onion starts to caramelize, add the carrots and cook for 4 minutes.
- ✓ After that, mix the water, brown sugar, and maple syrup. The sugars are prevented from burning by the addition of water.
- ✓ Finally, add the butter.

CHOCOLATE MUFFINS WITH HOT CHOCOLATE CUSTARD

Ingredients

- One tablespoon of cocoa powder
- Half tablespoon of bicarbonate soda
- 50g of golden-caster sugar
- 100g self rising flour
- 1 egg
- Two tablespoon of sunflower oil
- Four hot chocolate custard
- 25g dark chocolate (chopped)
- Low-fat custard

- ✓ Preheat oven to 160°C/140°F/gas 3 Using a drop of oil, brush the 6 holes of a muffin pan.
- ✓ In a big mixing cup, sieve the cocoa and add the remaining dry ingredients.
- ✓ Stir to combine, then build a well in the middle.
- ✓ In a jug, combine the milk, egg, and oil. Pour into the well and quickly stir to form a batter.
- ✓ Fill muffin tins halfway with batter, then bake for 15 minutes, or until risen and firm to the touch.
- ✓ Microwave the custard, then add the chopped chocolate and whisk

until smooth. Place the puddings
in bowls and top with the custard.

CHICKEN BUTTER BEAN AND LEEK PIE

Ingredients

- Two large boneless and skinless chicken breasts (cubed)
- One tablespoon of oil
- 420g of tin butter beans, drained and rinsed
- 10g of vegetable oil spread
- 2 leeks (sliced)
- 750g of floury potatoes, (cooked and mashed together)
- Two tablespoons of fresh tarragon (chopped)

- Two tablespoons of flour
- 50g of mature cheddar (grated)
- 600g of semi—skimmed milk

Instructions

- ✓ Preheat the oven to 200°C/gas 6 and heat the oil in a saucepan. Add the chicken and leeks and cook for 3-4 minutes, or until the chicken begins to brown.\
- ✓ Stir in the flour and 450ml milk, then bring to a boil, stirring constantly until the sauce thickens.
- ✓ Season with salt and pepper and stir in the tarragon, half of the cheese, and the butter beans.
- ✓ Place in an oven-safe bowl.
- ✓ Combine the mashed potatoes, remaining milk, butter, and

remaining cheese in a piping or spooning bag and pipe or spoon over the chicken mixture.

✓ Cook the pie in the oven for 19-24 minutes, or until golden and bubbly.

CHILLED PIZZA

Ingredients

- One teaspoon oregano
- Two sundried tomatoes (finely chopped)
- Four small plain naan breads (65g each)
- One red pepper (sliced)
- One yellow pepper (sliced)
- Ten fresh basil leaves (torn)

- Eight cherry tomatoes (quartered)

- Black pepper

- One teaspoon of rapeseed oil

- One red onion

- 30g light cream cheese (with garlic and herbs)

- 30g of cottage cheese

- One teaspoon of rapeseed oil

- One red onion

Instructions

- ✓ Preheat the oven to 190 degrees Celsius (gas 5) and pour the oil into a baking tray. Bake the onions and peppers for 14–18 minutes, or until they begin to brown.

- ✓ Remove the onions and peppers from the oven and set aside. Combine the oregano and sundried tomatoes in a mixing bowl. Remove from the oven and set aside to cool.

✓ Set aside the naan breads after baking them according to the package instructions (3–4 minutes).

✓ Spread cream cheese on each naan and dot with cottage cheese after the naan bread and vegetables have cooled for about 28 minutes.

✓ Scatter half of the basil leaves, the roasted peppers, and the onions over the top.

✓ Serve with a strong grind of black pepper on top of the tomatoes and the remaining basil leaves..

TURKEY AND PARSNIP CURRY

Ingredients

- Five tablespoons of madras curry paste
- 500g parsnip (peeled and cut into chunks)
- Two onions (thinly sliced)
- Two tablespoons of vegetable oil
- 500g of boneless turkey (cut into chunks)
- 400 gram can of chopped tomatoes
- 150 gram pot of low fat natural yogurt
- Cooked basmati rice (to serve)

Instructions

- ✓ Heat the oil in a saucepan, then add the onions and fry gently for 8 minutes, or until softened and lightly colored. Stir in the parsnips thoroughly.

✓ Stir in the curry paste, then add the tomatoes, along with a pinch of salt, and stir well. Get the one and half can of water to a boil.

✓ Reduce the heat to medium, cover, and cook for 15-18 minutes, or until the parsnips are tender.

✓ Finally, stir in the turkey bits, cover the grill, and cook for another 5 minutes, or until the turkey is thoroughly cooked. Remove from the heat source.

✓ Allow to cool completely before swirling in the yogurt and serving with basmati rice.

CHEEGAY OF FISH

Ingredients

- Black pepper (Freshly ground)

- 5cm piece of dried seaweed

- Two spring onions(sliced)

- One teaspoon of red miso

- Two shiitake mushrooms (sliced)

- Fish or vegetable stock(400ml)

- Cod fillet, cubed(250g)

- One teaspoon sesame oil

- Baby leaf spinach(250g)

- Chinese leaves (chopped)

Instructions

- ✓ Season the fish with salt and pepper, then drizzle with sesame oil.
- ✓ Cook for 3–6 minutes with the seaweed, spring onion, mushroom, and stock.
- ✓ Place the remaining ingredients in a saucepan and cook for 2–4 minutes, or until the fish and vegetables are done. Serve the food.

APPLE AND CINNAMON CAKE

Ingredients

- Three tablespoons of skimmed milk

- One kilogram of apple
- One heaped tablespoon of artificial granulated sweetener
- Three eggs
- One level teaspoon of ground cinnamon
- Baking powder(
- whole meal flour (100grams)
- vegetable oil based spread, melted (75grams)

Instructions

- ✓ Preheat the oven to 200°C/gas 6
- ✓ Sieve the flour into a mixing bowl, then stir in the artificial sweetener, baking powder, and cinnamon.
- ✓ In the center of the dry ingredients, make a well and pour in the eggs and milk. Apply the

melted butter to the whisked mixture.

- ✓ Apples should be peeled, cored, and seeds removed. Using a large knife, cut them into large slices. Fold in the apple slices gently into the mixture.
- ✓ Using vegetable oil, grease a cake pan. Bake for 33 minutes after pouring the mixture into the tin.
- ✓ Place on a cooling rack to cool. Allow to cool before serving.

BEEF GOULASH

Ingredients

- 1 x 200grams can tomatoes(chopped)
- One teaspoon of paprika

- One tablespoon of tomato puree
- 250grams lean braising steak (cubed)
- New potatoes (250g)
- Two teaspoons seasoned whole meal flour
- 150ml reduced salt beef stock or pork
- Half red pepper(chopped)
- One clove garlic (crushed)
- One teaspoon of oil
- One onion (chopped)

Instructions

- ✓ Preheat the oven to 180°C/160°C fan/gas mark 4 (180°C/160°C fan/gas mark 4).
- ✓ Toss the steak in the seasoned flour and set aside. Heat the oil in a flameproof casserole dish, then

add the steak and cook for 2 minutes, or until browned all over.

✓ Bring the remaining ingredients to a boil, then cover and place in the oven to keep warm. Cook until the meat is tender, about 1.5–2 hours.

✓ Serve with a variety of vegetables.

CORN AND PARMESAN MINI MUFFINS

Ingredients

- Two teaspoons of fresh rosemary (chopped)
- One tablespoon of baking powder
- Two eggs (beaten)
- Semi-skimmed milk (350ml)

- Vegetable oil based spread, melted (75grams)
- Whole meal flour(250grams)
  Fine polenta(250grams)
- One teaspoon paprika
- Two tablespoons of fresh Parmesan cheese (grated)

Instructions

- ✓ Preheat the oven to 200 degrees Celsius/gas 6.
- ✓ Grease some mini muffin tins lightly. You will need to re-use the muffin tins because the mixture makes 45 mini muffins, or you can make around 18 big muffins if you prefer.
- ✓ Combine the rice, polenta, baking powder, and paprika in a mixing dish.

✓ In a separate cup, whisk together the milk, butter, and eggs before folding into the flour mixture. Combine the bacon and rosemary in a mixing bowl.

✓ Spoon into muffin tins and top with a sprinkling of Parmesan cheese.

✓ Preheat oven to 375°F and bake for 6–9 minutes, or until golden. Allow to cool before serving.

CARROT CAKE

- Sultanas (50g)
- Carrots
- Two teaspoons of mixed spice
- Whole meal flour(300g)
- One teaspoon of baking powder
- Three eggs, beaten
- one banana,(mashed)

- Three tablespoons of granulated sweetener

- 50ml rapeseed oil + 2 teaspoons to oil the tin

For the topping:

- Walnut pieces (20g)

- One tablespoon of granulated sweetener

- Fat-free quark, 250g (cream cheese)

- Zest of one orange

Instructions

- ✓ Preheat the oven to 180°C/gas 4 and grease a 20cm x 25cm cake tin lightly with rapeseed oil.

- ✓ In a mixing bowl, combine the flour, baking powder, and spices.

- ✓ In a separate cup, whisk together the egg and banana. Combine the sweetener and oil in a mixing bowl.
- ✓ Fold the dry ingredients into the banana, egg, and oil mixture in a slow and steady motion, then fold in the sultanas and carrots.
- ✓ Fill a cake tin halfway with the mixture and bake for 24-30 minutes. Remove from the oven and cool on a wire rack.
- ✓ When the cake has cooled, spread the sweetened quark on top and sprinkle with walnuts and orange zest.

CHEESE, ONION AND SPINACH SCONES

Ingredients

- Good pinch white pepper
- Four spring onions (chopped finely)
- One teaspoon baking powder
- 75ml of skimmed milk
- Mature grated cheddar cheese (50g)
- Whole meal flour (200g)
- 75g of frozen spinach (defrosted and chopped finely)
- Two tablespoons of rapeseed oil
- Half teaspoon of paprika

Instructions

- ✓ Preheat the oven to 180°C/gas 4 and place a wide baking sheet inside.
- ✓ Combine the flour, baking powder, and pepper in a mixing bowl. Stir in the spinach and spring onion, then uniformly spread the grated cheese.
- ✓ Make a well in the center of the mixture and pour in the oil and half of the milk, mixing well with each addition. Continue adding the remaining milk until you have a soft yet strong dough.
- ✓ Roll the dough out 2cm thick on a lightly floured surface. Scones should be cut out with a medium cutter and placed on a hot oven

tray. To make an extra couple of scones, gather some scraps and roll out again.

- ✓ Glaze the tops with the remaining milk and top each scone with a little cheese and paprika (if using).
- ✓ Preheat oven to 350°F and bake for 12-15 minutes, or until golden brown.

CHICKEN BALTI

Ingrdients

- One tablespoon of tomato purée
- 25g of fresh coriander (chopped)
- Two skinless chicken breasts, (cubed)

- Two carrots (chopped)
- One heaped tsp garam masala
- One stick celery
- Four cloves garlic (crushed)
- One teaspoon rapeseed oil
- One onion, chopped
- Two to three heaped tsp curry powder
- One green pepper (chopped)
- One green chilli (sliced into rings)
- Tin chopped tomatoes

Instructions

- ✓ In a skillet, heat the oil, then add the onion and cook for 2–3 minutes, until softened. Cook for 2–3 minutes after adding the chicken.

- ✓ Cook for 2–3 minutes, stirring constantly, after adding the pepper, carrot, and celery.
- ✓ Stir in the garlic, curry powder, and garam masala until it is well coated in the spices.
- ✓ Bring to a gentle boil with the chilli, onions, and tomato purée.
- ✓ Cover and cook for 11–13 minutes, or until carrots are tender. Serve after mixing in the coriander.

CHICKPEA AND TUNA SALAD

Ingredients

- Extra-virgin olive oil (2ml)
- Two lemon wedges
- Grated zest of half a lemon

- Salad leaves/lettuce
- A pinch of black pepper
- One small red onion (finely chopped)
- Tin chickpeas in water, drained
- Ripe cherry tomatoes, cut into quarters(180g)
- Cucumber, chopped
- Tin tuna in water, drained (drained weight 150g)

Instructions

- ✓ In a large mixing bowl, combine the lemon zest, pepper, and olive oil; add the red onion, tomatoes, and cucumber; mix well, and set aside for a few minutes to infuse.
- ✓ Fold in the chickpeas and tuna gently so that it is evenly covered in the dressing.

✓ Finally, add the salad leaves and split between two lunch boxes, along with a lemon wedge to squeeze over the top before eating.

COCONUT RICE PUDDING

Ingredients

- One tablespoon toasted coconut
- Few drops vanilla essence
- Basmati rice (100grams)
- One tablespoon of toasted coconut
- Soya milk(300ml)
- Unsweetened coconut milk drink(400ml)
- Granulated sweetener (25g)

Instructions

✓ In a small pan, combine all of the ingredients, except the toasted coconut. Reduce the heat to low and cook for 22–25 minutes, or until the rice is tender.

✓ Serve with toasted coconut on top.

COWBOY-STYLE PORK AND BEANS

Ingredients

- Two medium onions (finely chopped)
- One tablespoon of tomato puree
- One teaspoon of blackstrap molasses
- One red pepper, finely chopped
- Two cloves garlic, chopped

- Two teaspoons rapeseed oil
- Pork fillet (400g)
- tin cannellini beans, drained (2 x 400grams)
- Tin chopped tomatoes (2 x 400grams)
- One heaped teaspoon (smoked paprika)
- One teaspoon chilli powder

Instructions

- ✓ In a saucepan, heat the oil, then add the onions and cook for 2-4 minutes.
- ✓ Cook for another 2 minutes after adding the red pepper and garlic.
- ✓ Cook for 3-4 minutes, or until the pork is browned.
- ✓ Simmer for 15 minutes after adding the chopped tomatoes,

puree, molasses, paprika, and chili.

✓ Stir in the beans and cook for another 5 minutes before serving.

CRANNBERRY SAUCE

Ingredients

- Three tablespoons port
- Grated rind and juice of one orange
- Intense sweetener or sugar to taste
- Fresh cranberries(350g)
- fresh cranberries (350g)

Instructions

✓ In a pan, combine the cranberries, port, orange rind, and juice.

- ✓ Cover and cook for 7–10 minutes, until they are softened and juicy.
- ✓ To taste, add more sweetener or sugar.
- ✓ Cool and chill until you're ready to use it.

19. DONER KEBABS

Ingredients

- One egg (lightly beaten)
- 10% of fat minced lamb
- One teaspoon of ground cinnamon
- Half teaspoon of ground cumin
- One heaped teaspoon oregano
- Half teaspoon chilli flakes
- Grated zest and juice of half lemon

- Half slice of whole meal bread
  (crumbled)
- A pinch of white pepper
- Juice of half lemon (for serving)
- Two cloves garlic (crushed)
- Four whole meal pitta breads
- Four large servings salad

Instructions

- ✓ In a mixing bowl, combine the
  oregano, cinnamon, cumin, chili,
  pepper, garlic, lemon zest, and
  juice, as well as the egg and
  crumbled bread.
- ✓ With a fork, thoroughly combine
  the ingredients, breaking up the
  bread even further.
- ✓ In a separate bowl, combine the
  lamb and set aside for 10 minutes.
  Mix again, then form into a loaf

with a diameter of 6cm and a length of 13.5cm. Cook for 25–30 minutes on a baking sheet at 190°C/gas 5 in a preheated oven.

✓ Allow to cool for 5 minutes before slicing thinly and stuffing into pita breads with salad. Serve with a squeeze of lemon juice.

GAMMON AND PINEAPPLE STIR FRY

Ingredients

- Two tablespoon tomato purée
- Chestnut mushrooms, sliced (115grams)
- Can pineapple chunks in natural juice
- Freshly ground black pepper

- 200g gammon steak, all visible fat
  and rind removed
- One red pepper, seeded and sliced
- One tablespoon of cider vinegar
- 225g of bean sprouts
- Eight spring onions (finely sliced)

Instructions

- ✓ Using a sharp knife, cut the
  gammon into thin strips.
- ✓ A nonstick wok should be heated.
  Cook for 3 minutes over high heat
  with the gammon.
- ✓ Cook for 1 minute after adding the
  sliced spring onions, pepper, and
  mushrooms.
- ✓ Drain the pineapple juice and
  combine it with the vinegar and
  tomato purée in a mixing bowl.

✓ Pour the sauce over the pineapple chunks and bean sprouts that have been added to the wok.

✓ Bring to a boil, tossing well. Serve right out of the pan.

SAUSAGE AND BACON OMELETTE

Ingredients

- Cooking spray (Calorie-controlled)
- Two lean chicken sausages
- Two lean bacon medallions
- 75g of cherry tomatoes (halved)
- One tablespoon of spicy tomato chutney
- One teaspoon lemon juice
- Handful rocket leaves

- Two eggs
- Skimmed milk (50ml)

Instructions

- ✓ Set a large nonstick frying pan over medium-high heat and spray it with cooking spray. Cook the sausages and bacon for 5 minutes, turning once.
- ✓ Cook for 2 minutes after adding the tomatoes. Remove the sausages from the heat and cut them in half lengthwise.
- ✓ In a mixing bowl, combine the rocket and lemon juice, season to taste, and set aside.
- ✓ In a jug, whisk together the eggs and milk, then season.
- ✓ Set a small nonstick frying pan over medium-high heat, lightly

misted with cooking spray. Pour in the egg mixture and cook for 25-30 seconds, or until the omelette's base is set.

✓ Draw the omelette's edges into the center with a spatula to allow any uncooked egg to pass underneath. as well as chutney

✓ Cook for 3-4 minutes more, or until almost set.

✓ Place the sausages, bacon, and tomatoes on half of the omelette and fold the omelette over to enclose the filling.

✓ Transfer to a plate and top with rocket and chutney.

CHICKEN SQUASH AND CORIANDER PILA

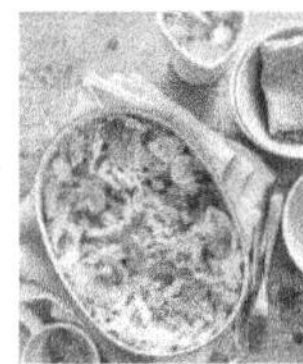

Ingredients

- Two teaspoons of sunflower oil
- Nine oz wholegrain rice
- Two teaspoons of mild curry powder
- Ground cumin(1 teaspoon)
- One teaspoon ground coriander
- Half teaspoon of ground turmeric
- Two tablespoon flaked almonds
- 750 ml of water
- One yellow/green courgette, thinly sliced
- Freshly ground black pepper

- Two large skinless chicken breasts (400g)
- Half lemon (juiced)
- One handful of coriander leaves

Instructions

- ✓ Preheat the oven to 180°C (160° fan)/350°F/gas mark 4 and heat the sunflower oil until hot in an ovenproof casserole or baking dish placed over a medium heat.
- ✓ Stir in the rice and cook for 2 minutes in the oil, stirring frequently. Cook for an additional 2-3 minutes, or until the spices are fragrant.
- ✓ Cover with water and stir thoroughly. Before placing the squash and chicken on top of the rice, bring to a boil.

- ✓ Cover the dish loosely with aluminum foil and bake for about 28 minutes, or until the rice has absorbed the liquid and the chicken is cooked through.
- ✓ Remove the foil from the oven and set it aside.
- ✓ Return the dish to the oven for an additional 8-10 minutes, or until the almonds are golden brown.
- ✓ Remove the baking sheet from the oven. Place the chicken on a plate and set aside for 5 minutes to cool before shredding with two forks.
- ✓ To separate the grains, add some lemon juice to the pilaf and fluff the rice with a fork.

- ✓ Until serving, top with the shredded chicken and some coriander leaves.

POTATO AND LENTIL CURRY

Ingredients

- One teaspoon of sunflower oil
- One onion, chopped
- One teaspoon of mustard seeds
- One teaspoon chilli powder
- One teaspoon ground coriander
- One pinch turmeric
- Six tablespoons of fresh coriander leaves
- Chopped tomatoes (200g)
- Two tablespoon of tomato purée
- Fresh ginger (peeled and grated)

- 125g of yellow lentils(washed and drained)
- Vegetable stock (600ml)
- Floury potatoes,(900g peeled and cubed)
- Fresh coriander leaves

Instructions

- ✓ In a medium saucepan, heat the sunflower oil.
- ✓ Fry for 3 minutes after adding the onion. Continue to fry for 1 minute after adding the mustard seeds, ginger, chili powder, coriander, turmeric, and fresh coriander.
- ✓ Pour the stock over the tomatoes, tomato puree, and lentils in the pan.
- ✓ Bring to a boil, then reduce heat to low, cover, and cook for 25-30

minutes, or until lentils are almost tender.

- ✓ Stir in the potatoes and cook for another 10-15 minutes, or until they are tender.
- ✓ Serve with raita made from yogurt and coriander leaves.

FRENCH ONION SOUP

Ingredients

- One teaspoon low-salt soy sauce
- Three teaspoons sunflower oil
- Sweet potatoes(400grams)
- One low-salt vegetable stock cube
- Twenty grams reduced-fat mature Cheddar cheese
- Twenty grams mozzarella

- One tablespoon fresh parsley, finely chopped.

- 1kg onions (finely chopped)

- Four slices of whole meal bread

- A good pinch pepper

Instructions

- ✓ Preheat the oven to 190 degrees Celsius/gas 5.
- ✓ In a saucepan, heat 2 teaspoons of the oil, then add the onions and cook, stirring constantly, for 30–40 minutes, until the onions caramelize.
- ✓ Place the remaining oil on a baking sheet while the onions are caramelizing. Muddle the potatoes in the mixture until they are

evenly coated, then bake for 30–
35 minutes.

✓ Add the stock to the onions, bring
to a boil, and then reduce to a low
heat for 5 minutes.

✓ Meanwhile, to make the cheesy
croutons: Grill each half-slice of
bread, then turn over and top with
the Cheddar cheese and
mozzarella, then grill until the
cheese melts and browns.

✓ Alternatively, place the cheese-
topped bread on a baking sheet
and bake for 5-10 minutes.

✓ Pour the soup into four bowls and
stir in the parsley, pepper, and soy
sauce.

✓ Serve with sweet potato wedges on
the side, as well as cheesy croutons

and a sprinkling of fresh parsley
on top.

BARLEY AND WILD MUSHROOM

Ingredients

- Four tablespoon oat/soya-based
  cream as alternative
- Good grind of black pepper
- One onion (140grams), chopped
- One red pepper (160grams),
  chopped
- pearl barley (250grams)
- Two teaspoons olive oil
- 400g of mixed mushrooms (sliced)
- Two pinches white pepper
- One low-salt vegetable stock cube
  in 700ml of boiling water

- Two cloves of garlic, crushed
- One heaped teaspoon of dried oregano
- One heaped teaspoon of chopped fresh basil

Instructions

- ✓ In a large nonstick frying pan, heat the oil, then add the onion and cook for 1 minute.
- ✓ Cook for 2 minutes with the red pepper and garlic, then add the mushrooms and cook for 3 minutes.
- ✓ Set aside a few mushrooms to use as a garnish.
- ✓ Stir in the barley, then add the stock, oregano, and pepper, and combine thoroughly. Bring to a boil, then reduce to a low heat,

cover, and cook, stirring constantly.

✓ Remove the cover after about 25 minutes and continue to simmer for another 10 minutes, or until the liquid has been absorbed and any excess has been boiled off.

✓ Cook the barley until it is tender but still firm ('al dente').

✓ Stir in the cream substitute and fresh basil, then season to taste with freshly ground black pepper and the reserved basil and mushrooms.

BREAD SAUCE

Ingredients

- 125g of fresh eight peppercorns

- 10g of vegetable oil spread
- Whole meal breadcrumbs
- One medium onion, peeled
- 600ml of whole milk
- Ten cloves
- One bay leaf

Instructions

- ✓ Using the cloves to pierce the onion, put it in a pan with the milk, bay leaf, and peppercorns.
- ✓ Bring to a low simmer, then remove from the heat and set aside for 2 hours to let the flavors evolve.

LEEK AND POTATO SALAD

- One heaped teaspoon Dijon mustard
- Good pinch of white pepper
- 25g parsley
- 0% of fat Greek yogurt
- Baby new potatoes(600grams)
- One large leek (250grams)finely sliced
- 10g of chives

Instructions

- ✓ Cook the potatoes whole for 18-20 minutes, or until they are just tender. Set aside after a quick rinse in cold water.
- ✓ Meanwhile, combine the leeks, yogurt, chives and parsley,

mustard, and pepper in a mixing bowl.

✓ To ensure that all of the leeks are coated, mix it together thoroughly. Refrigerate until ready to use.

✓ When the potatoes are cool enough to handle, cut them in half and toss with the yogurt dressing and more herbs.

SCARY SOUP WITH TOMBSTONE BREAD

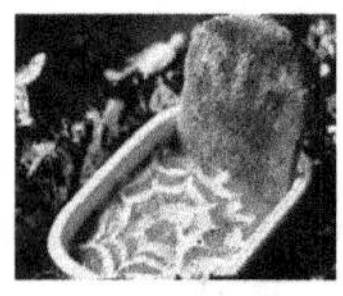

Ingredients

- Good pinch pepper
- 75g of red lentils
- Two teaspoons rapeseed oil
- One low salt vegetable stock cube

- 400g of can tomatoes

- One tablespoon tomato puree

- One large onion, chopped

- One small butternut squash (500g prepared weight)

- Four slices whole meal bread

Instructions

- ✓ Using 1 teaspoon of oil, add the onion to the pan. Cook, stirring occasionally, until the onion starts to brown.

- ✓ Simmer for 18-20 minutes after adding the squash, stock, lentils, tomatoes, and puree.

- ✓ Add a strong pinch of pepper, then blend or process until smooth with a stick blender or in a food processor.

- ✓ Meanwhile, cut the bread into a tombstone shape, place the stencil in place, and spray the toasted bread.
- ✓ Into bowls, ladle the soup. Fill a piping bag with the yoghurt and a very small nozzle, and pipe a thin spiral onto the soup.
- ✓ To make a spider's web, draw a skewer or chopstick through the spiral from the center outwards. After that, add the toast.

ROASTED CHOICORY AND ORANGE SALAD

Ingredients

- One teaspoon fresh thyme or pinch dried

- Black pepper (Freshly ground)
- Four heads of chicory
- Grated rind and juice of one orange
- one teaspoon of olive oil
- Two oranges, segmented
- Two teaspoons orange zest, to garnish

Instructions

- ✓ Preheat the oven to 200 degrees Celsius/gas 6.
- ✓ In an ovenproof bowl, position the chicory. Combine the orange rind and juice, oil, and thyme in a mixing bowl. Season with plenty of black pepper and sprinkle over the chicory.

- ✓ Cook for 28-30 minutes, or until they are tender and starting to char.
- ✓ Toss with the orange segments and serve with some cooking liquid and orange zest drizzled on top. Allow to cool slightly or chill before serving.

BUTTERBEAN PATE

Ingredients

- 400g can butterbeans, drained
- Four spring onions, finely chopped (50g)
- 6cm cucumber(finely diced)
- Two tablespoons of low-fat natural yogurt

- One clove of garlic, crushed
- One tablespoon of extra-virgin olive oil
- juice and zest of half lemon
- three sprigs of fresh mint, chopped
- A pinch of pepper
- A pinch of paprika
- Four cherry tomatoes
- One stick celery (cut into batons)
- half bulb fennel (cut into batons)
- one large carrot(cut into batons)
- one yellow pepper (cut into batons)
- mixed crudites

Instructions

- ✓ Half of the beans should be thoroughly mashed with a fork until fully smooth. Combine the two halves after lightly crushing the other half.
- ✓ Set aside after mixing in the spring onions, cucumber, yogurt, garlic, olive oil, lemon, mint, and pepper.
- ✓ Prepare the vegetable sticks for dipping in the meantime.
- ✓ Re-mix the pâté, then top with paprika and serve.

Conclusion

Food can be effective in the prevention and reversal of diabetes. Nevertheless, nutritional practices have improved as we know more about the condition. The conventional diabetes approach focuses on reducing the processed sugars and foods that release enough sugars during digestion such as starches, breads, bananas, etc. The diet can contain an excessive amount of fat and protein, with reduced carbohydrates. Diabetes specialists have therefore taken precautions to restrict fat-especially saturated fats that can increase cholesterol levels, and to restrict protein for people with compromised kidney function. The new strategy relies more on the fat. Fat is a problem for diabetes sufferers. The more fat the diet produces, the longer it takes for insulin to get glucose into the cells. By comparison, lowering fat consumption and reducing body fat make insulin do much more than it does.

In Summary, effective lifestyle modifications include weight loss therapy, implementation of a healthy dietary pattern such as the Mediterranean diet, along with physical activity are the foundation of type 2 diabetes prevention. Therefore, emphasis needs to be placed on promoting a healthier lifestyle and seeking solutions to enhance commitment and adherence to lifestyle modifications, particularly for people at high risk.

People with uncontrolled diabetes will experience fatigue , nausea, constant urination and blurred vision in the short run. In the long term, they are at risk for heart failure, renal complications, eye defects, nerve loss and other issues.

But remember that diabetics is not a death sentence, You can therefore treat or suspend diabetes by healthy eating , exercise, weight control, medications and also through prayers. **I wish you quick and perfect recovery.**